Off-Grid Guide.

Survival Reference When There's Nowhere To Run

Disclamer: All photos used in this book, including the cover photo were made available under a <u>Attribution-ShareAlike 2.0 Generic (CC BY-SA 2.0)</u>

and sourced from <u>Flickr</u>

Table of Contents

Introduction

There you are, living your ordinary life, doing your ordinary thing. You wake up, you go to work, and you spend your day slaving away, then you go home. You do the normal things you do in your evening, then you go to bed.

You think this is the way things are going to be forever. You don't really do much else, and you don't really dream of doing much else. All you think of is what you are going to do the next day, how you are going to make it through the next week, and how you are going to manage your next hour.

Then it happens.

You don't know what it is. You didn't see it coming... it just happens. Perhaps it's a flood, or a tornado, or some sort of tropical storm. Perhaps it's an earthquake, or perhaps the country suddenly goes under attack and the area you live in is the area that took the brunt of the hit.

Perhaps you are suddenly forced out of your home, off of your land, and into the great unknown. You have to head out of town, heading for somewhere else that is safer. Somewhere higher, or lower, somewhere dryer or somewhere away from all of the danger.

You have to get out, and you don't know where you are headed.

"Where can I go? Where is there to go when something like this happens?"

"What am I going to do if I have to stay out here long term?"

"How am I going to manage if I am stuck out here for months?"

All these thoughts and fears rush through your mind, and you are not alone. Whenever anything like this happens, you are bound to be scared, but with the right skills, you are going to be fine. Just fine.

Let me show you what you need to do to pull through when something like this happens. Let me show you how to keep things together when the world is falling apart, and let me show you how you can be the beacon that everyone turns to when everything seems to be hopeless and lost.

This book is going to change the way you view disaster, and it is going to help you be that calm and collected one when things seem to fall completely apart. This book is going to be exactly what you need when you have to get out of dodge.

Learn the skills, and keep it together.

You will be just fine.

Chapter 1 – Getting Out of Town

Often, when you see people having to get out of town quickly, you see them get in their cars and simply drive out of town. In the movies, when you this happening, you see all kinds of different things happening, from them having to drive around accidents, drive through natural disasters, or dodging all kinds of various obstacles on the road.

We often make the mistake of thinking that we would be able to do this exact same thing if we were in that same situation, but the fact of the matter is that you may not be able to use your car at all.

What would you do if a flash flood suddenly rendered all roads impassable?

What about if you were to try to get out of the city, but you discover that the main roads are blocked and there's no way around them?

What would you do if you were waiting for help to arrive, but no one came to help, or there was no way for anyone to come help?

All of these situations, though they aren't what you want to think about, are feasible, and you have to be ready to handle them if they do happen.

No matter where you live, there are designated routes you can follow to get out of town. Learn the map of your area, and learn what routes you can take to get out of town if you ever need to quickly

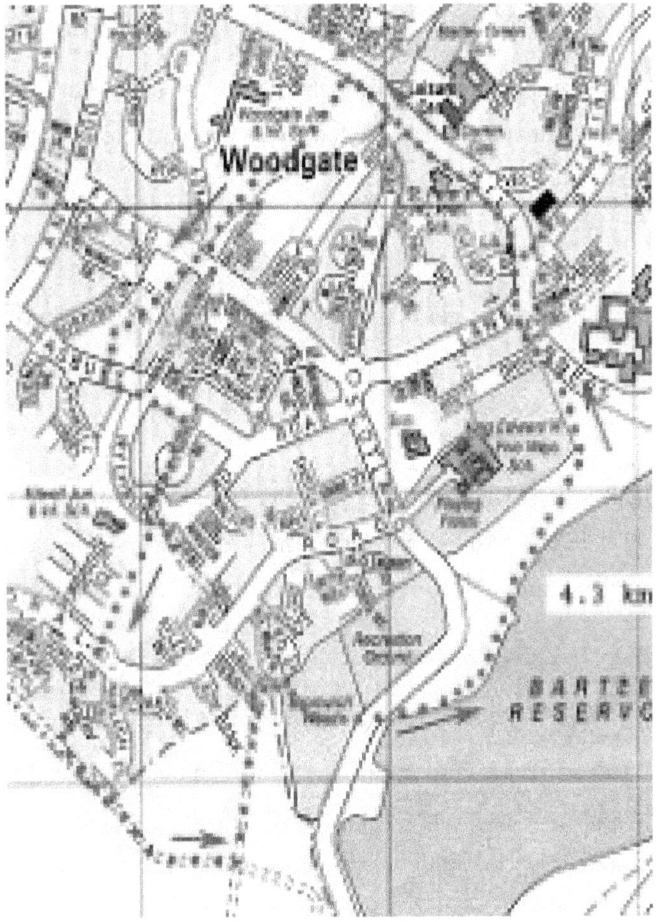

Don't just stick with the main roads, but also look into the side roads, the back roads, and the trails you can take if you have to. Look at walking paths that run through the town and head out of town, and look at the bite routes you can take if it comes to that.

When you have to get out, you need to be ready for anything, including what you will do if you don't have access to a vehicle, or you can't gain access to transportation.

As you know, your bug-out bag should be light enough for you to carry it over long distances, and for you to move quickly with it. Make it as portable as possible, and you won't have an issue.

In addition to knowing how to get out of town, you need to be able to get out quickly.

You never know what's going to happen, and if your city were to suddenly be under attack, suddenly placed in the direct route of a tornado or some other natural disaster, or for any other reason you had to get you, you want to do it as quickly as possible.

The best way to get faster at this is to practice. Time yourself to gauge how long it takes you now right now, then practice to cut back on that time. If you are in the center of town, you need to practice until you can get out on foot in under half an hour.

If you are on the outskirts, you want to be able to not only get out quickly, but to get out and get started on the path to where you are going quickly.

Set up options in various places, so you know what to plan on when the time comes.

Decide if you are going to have connections in other towns, decide if you are going to keep modes of transportation in various places, and decide where you are going to head after you are out of town.

Depending on where you live, you can stay in the area, or you can head out to a safer place. Decide in advance what is going to cause you to move to a different area, and prepare in advance what you need to do.

The goal is to be able to get out of where you are quickly, in spite of what you are in town and what you need to bring with you.

Chapter 2 – Out of the Frying Pan

As a general rule of thumb, most people think that when things go bad, they are going to either drive to the nearest designated area, or they are going to get on the safety bus and head out of town that way.

The problem with this mindset is that there may not always be somewhere for you to go, or something to take you to get there. This is going to lead to a variety of issues if, for some reason, this isn't an option. So, it is always a good idea to know where you should go if things were to suddenly go south.

This is bound to make you wonder where you can go if things were to suddenly go wrong

No matter where you live, it's really only a matter of time before things do go wrong. It may not be in your lifetime, it may not have been in your parent's or their parent's lifetimes, but in the world we live, it's just a matter of time before you need to know how to get out of danger, and where to go when it happens.

Now, of course everywhere on the planet has drawbacks and things you have to watch out for, but there are definitely places on the planet that are safer than others. Since we are here in America, we are going to focus on the places here at home that are safer, as well as some of the places in our neighboring countries.

I realize that some areas are out of range for you to get to, and there are others that are going to take some time to get to, but if you prepare, you are going to be able to get to them without any real issue.

Let's take a minute to look at where these areas are on the map, and form some solid ideas on how you can get to them if you ever need to.

Zone 1

While there are no actually designated zones in the United States, I am going to give you some now so you know where you go. You can call them what you want and decide where you would like to go if you ever need to, but simply use the zoning as a reference guide.

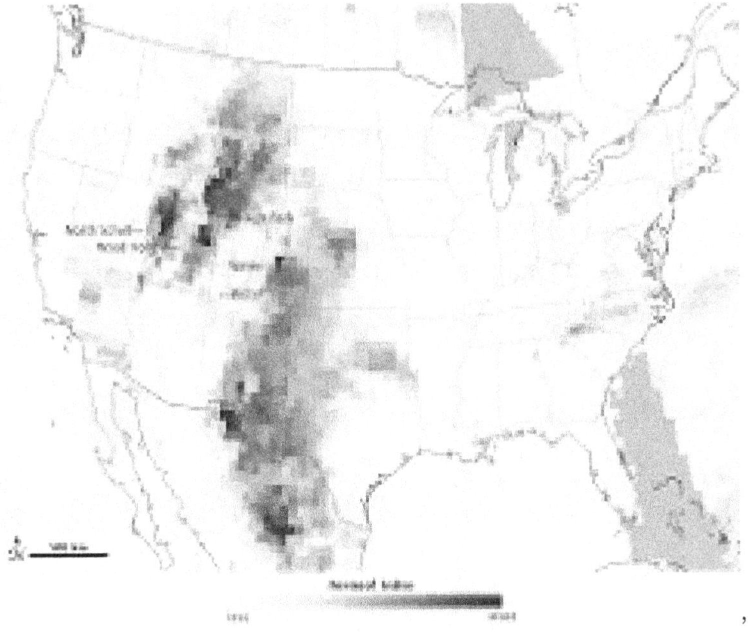

Zone 1 refers to the area in the western united states. It starts up in Oregon and on the downward side of the Sierra Mountain range, and lies on the Pacific side of the Rocky Mountains. It reaches clear down to the south, reaching almost to New Mexico.

The reason this is an ideal place is because these mountains form a natural barrier against forces coming from the eastern side. On the other side, you have the Pacific Ocean as a barrier.

Zone 2

Another option to head to is the Maine and New Hampshire area. This is far enough in the north that you don't have to worry about many of the tropical storms that those in the South face.

There is a range of protection further north from this area. Take note that this is only best if you are avoiding natural disasters. If you are trying to avoid something that has to do with war or attacks on the United States, then you will want to stay away from large cities or areas close to these large cities.

Zone 3

Not all places to run are in the United States. There are times that, even when you are in the United States, you are going to want to get out of the country. Getting out of the country may not be in your plans, but it's always good to have options for what you can do.

As far as Canada goes, you have many options for places to bug-out. When you are selecting an area, you need to factor in what is going on where you currently are, and what you are looking for in where you are going.

Canada is a wide area that is as almost as diverse as the United States. You have plenty of options to choose from when it comes to mountains and woods, plains and areas you can bunker down and wait things out.

Of course, this is also dependent on what you are looking to achieve in your safety zone. If you are looking for places you can hide out for a while, you will want to select places such as Canada, but if you are going for more open areas where you can start your own agriculture, you are going to be better off in areas such as the Rocky Mountains.

Keep in mind you don't have to have just one area to head when things go wrong, you can always be flexible and choose based on what is going on and what you need at the time

One of the biggest ways you can be ready for anything is to do just that... prepare for anything. You can't tell for sure what is coming, so you might have to wait until things actually happen before you decide for sure what your course of action is going to be.

In the chapters to come we are going to take a look at ways you can prepare to get up and go whenever the time comes, and how you can be entirely prepared for anything that happens.

Chapter 3 – Big City Issues

In this world we live in, most people prefer to live in large cities. Of course there are a lot of benefits to living in large cities, but there are also a number of drawbacks as well.

With the congestion of buildings, you gain a lot of convenience, but with that same congestion, you are going to run into problems when it comes to getting out of town.

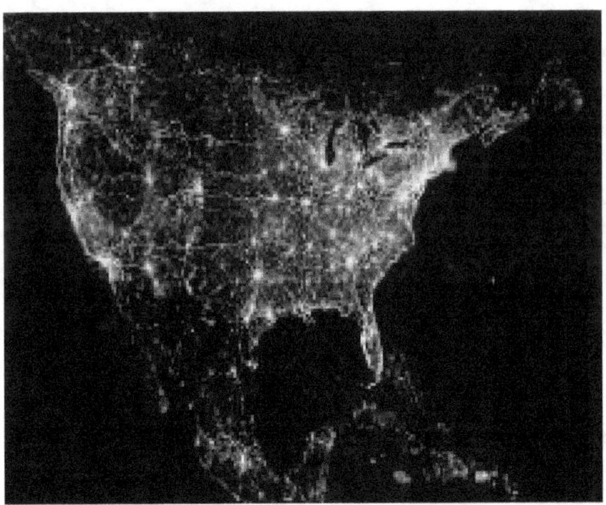

First of all, you are going to run into a higher risk of attack.

Sadly, the more people in an area make the area more prone to some form of attack from a foreign nation. While you don't want to live your life in fear of this happening, you do want to be ready for when it does.

Secondly, a lot of people in a small area is going to cause disease to spread a lot faster

Disease outbreaks aren't as common these days, but they still do happen. The more people you find in an area, the faster these are going to spread. This means you have to take more than one caution. Not only do you have to watch out for the outbreak itself, but you have to be careful of those that carry the disease with them as they leave the city.

If you are facing a natural disaster, a lot of people and buildings in one area can pose more dangers, as well as make it harder for you to get where you need to go

If you have to get out of the city, make sure you keep an eye out for other people running through the streets, you watch out for falling buildings or things falling off of buildings, and accidents that can happen from panicked drivers tearing through the streets.

The bigger the city, the longer it is going to take for you to get out of it

Don't trust the internet to tell you how long it takes for you to get out of an area. Do the trials yourself to determine the exact amount of time it's going to take you. The difference between how long it takes you to get out and how long you think it's going to take you could be the difference between life and death.

When it comes to any kind of survival situation, speed is of essence. You might be able to search how long it's supposed to take you to get out of an area, but unless you actually take the time to measure, you won't know for sure.

Also factor in that you have to account for the other people who are going to be on the road, the obstructions that are going to be in the way, and the panic that is going to be in the air.

You might have to also factor in bad weather, poor driving conditions or impass- able roadways, and other factors that could slow you down.

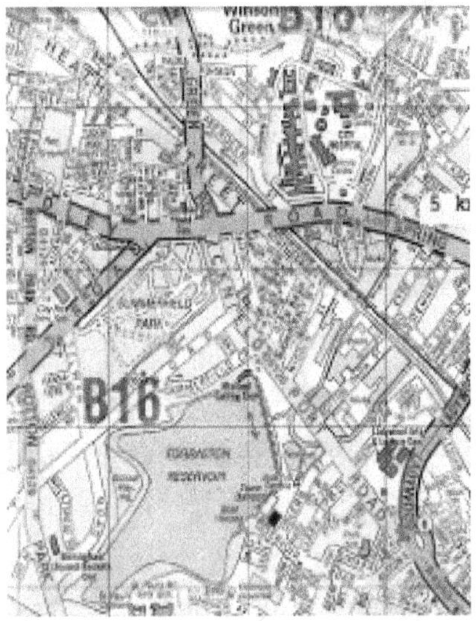

Injuries, the number of people in your party, and the various factors that will cause them to slow down or slow you down are more things you want to bring into your calculations

Odds are, you have family you are going to make sure gets out of town with you, whether that be your partner and children, your siblings, or your parents if they are older. You may also wish to bring pets depending on what you have.

If you are going to bring any pets, make sure you have your own supplies ready to grab when you have to get out. If you are taking an animal such as a dog or cat, make sure you know where they are going to be and where their things are.

I recommend you keep their supplies right next to your other bug-out supplies, and that you can get them quickly. It can be a hard decision to make, but when you are in a hurry, you have to grab things and go. When you have pets, you can't afford to spend a lot of time looking around for them, so make sure they are ready to go when you are.

Part of these preparations can include more than just your bag. Feel free to get a passport if you are going to head out of the country, keep money set aside if you are going to want to purchase a plane ticket.

There's no amount of money that will be the magic amount, but it never hurts to have some set aside for when you need it.

Try to keep at least a few hundred dollars aside if you can spare it, or save up over time. You may never need it, but if you ever do, you are going to need as much as you can spare.

You never know what's going to happen, and any supplies you have may be the only thing you have left in the world.

Chapter 4 – Living Off the Land

Up until now, we have been discussing the things you can do and the places you can go if you are needing to get out of the area you live in.

But leaving is only half the battle. Once you get where you are going, you need to have a plan for survival.

If you have a standard bug-out bag, you have roughly three days to live off of your bag. Of course, if you have bigger bags, you have a lot longer to live off out of the bag, but if you are only going with standard, you might need to figure out something else quickly.

Depending on your situation, if you end up in an open area, you are going to have to learn how to live off of the land itself, which you can do with most of the supplies you already have in your bag

If you keep the standard supplies in your bag, then you have the things you need to pitch a tent, to hunt for animals and prepare what you hunt for dinner, or even the things you need to plant edible food.

When it comes to living off the land, you have to start by choosing the right location. This is going to be an area that is safe, secure, and out of the elements.

Look for a place that gives you a bird's eye view of the layout of the land, look for a place that gives you access to the essentials you will need such as water and small game, and look for a place you can use long term if you have to.

For most natural disasters, you are going to be able to head back home within a few days, but if you are the victim of a major emergency, it could be months before you can head home again, if you ever can. If this is the case, you need to be selective over where you choose to settle down.

In addition to the standards you choose for your base camp, you need to keep a few more things in mind:

Staying away from cities is essential

Of course, you can stay close to small towns, especially if you are going to need more supplies. If you are still in the area of a large city, try to go the other direction for your supplies. Every large city on the map has a few smaller towns nearby, and it wouldn't be hard for you to settle down close to one of those.

Learn to distinguish friends from foes

Let's face it, people can get downright crazy when it comes to survival situations, and you don't want to get caught up in the wrong situation with the wrong kinds of people.

As a general rule of thumb, keep your distance as much as possible until you know for sure the kind of people you are interacting with. If you simply meet people, make sure you keep your supplies and valuables under wraps until you know for sure what they are after.

There's something about natural disasters and emergencies that makes everyone think only of themselves, and there's times this prompts people to behave in ways they normally wouldn't. This isn't to say that you can't trust anyone, in fact, you are going to want to find people who feel the same way as you if you are going to have to live this way long term.

But, finding people like you is a lot different than simply trusting every stranger you meet on the road.

Overall, a system of trust is always the best thing to embrace when you are in any form of survival situation, but you can't be too careful. If you can, try to form a group of people who are like minded and after the same things you are... this is going to give you all a better chance of pulling through anything you are facing

In other words, see what every person has to bring to the table. You are primarily focused on yourself, and how you can pull through this emergency, but that doesn't mean you can't band together with others along the way.

In the next chapter, we are going to take a look at how you can form these communities, as well as the best way to go about managing these kinds of situations. Again, preparation is the best key to survival, and the more you are ready for, the better off everyone is going to be.

Chapter 5 – Bug-Out Communities

If you take any time at all to browse the internet, it isn't going to take long before you realize you aren't alone in your preparation. Not only are there countless others online who are preparing for the same kinds of situations you are, but there are those that are also looking to build communities in these kinds of situations.

As I said in the last chapter, you can't trust everyone you run into on the road, but that doesn't mean there aren't going to be plenty of people out there that you can trust

In fact, I encourage you right now to take the time to form online friendships with people like this. Not only are you giving yourself a support system, but you are also giving yourself a community in the event a national emergency does happen in your lifetime.

If you prepare for this kind of community in advance, everyone is going to know what to expect of each other and themselves. If you know where you are all headed, what you are all able to bring along, and what your strengths are as individuals, you are going to be much better able to band together when you are in a survival situation.

Of course, you may not be lucky enough to find the same people in real life that you were chatting with online, but this doesn't mean that you shouldn't try. Not only is forming friendships like this online help you out if the situation were to arise, but it's going to help you prepare for if it ever does.

Obviously you are using resources such as this book to aid in your learning and preparation for any emergency, but the more people you talk to, the more ideas you can gather, and the more tips and tricks you can embrace

Approach everyone you meet as someone who has something useful to share with you, end store away all of the information you find. You never know who is going to give you that bit of advice that is going to change the way you view things, and you never know who you are going to inspire to do the same thing.

The more we band together and help each other, the better off we are going to be long term.

When this kind of emergency does happen, whether it happens to be an attack on the country of some sort of natural disaster, you can use this same principle with people you meet

Of course, this is talking for the long term. If you are only going to be out for a few days, you are going to be in a drastically different situation than if you are out for a few months or longer, but the point stays the same.

View other people as people who can help you, and see how you can help them. The more people you can get together, the more likely your chances for all of you surviving. We all openly assume we are going to be the ones who make it through anything we face, but in all honesty, when you are in a life or death situation, you have just as much a chance of not making it through as the next person does.

If you are able to bring a group of people together, you are going to be better able to take care of each other in a variety of ways.

If you are out there for the long term, work on forming a community that functions and helps each other.

You would be surprised at how much a few people can accomplish, especially if they are all under the same goal. If you are in a survival situation, and you find a group of people who are in the same boat, band together and get things done. Give everyone a job to do, and make sure everyone has a purpose.

One of the biggest issues people in general come across when they are in survival situations is that they forget they have a purpose in life, and they neglect to pursue that purpose. They let life slip away as something they used to live, and end up driving themselves crazy in the process.

If you maintain the same kind of life you did before, meaning you still have jobs to do, you still work to get the food you have, and you still maintain that sense of purpose, you are all going to be far better off than if you are all sitting around and waiting out whatever you are faced with.

Be proactive, and build a community. You are all going to have a place, and you are all going to work together to survive. If the danger passes and you are all able to go home, then you have succeeded in getting through the disaster together. If you are left out there for months at a time, then you are going to be grateful for each other and the work you are doing.

Either way, you are working together for the good, and you will see the results of this.

In the world we live in, it's only a matter of time before we are all faced with some sort of emergency, but the more we prepare, and the more we have each other, the more of us are going to make it through.

Conclusion

There you have it, everything you need to know to keep your world together when the rest of the world is falling apart. It's no secret that this isn't going to be fun, and you are going to have to work hard to keep it together when you are faced with any kind of natural disaster, but with this book, you are going to achieve the skills you need to make that happen.

I hope this book inspires you to be ready for anything. Never live your life in paranoia, but always live your life prepared. You never know what is going to happen, and the more prepared you are, the better.

The goal of this book is to make you prepared, and to keep you ready no matter what. Be ready for anything, whether it has to do with the weather, or whether you are dealing with something entirely different. Get ready to jump into the world of preparedness, and you are going to be ready, no matter what.

The world is unpredictable, but you have a handle on it, you just have to be ready.

FREE Bonus Reminder

If you have not grabbed it yet, please go ahead and download your special bonus report
"Preppers Survival Guide. Proven Tactics For Armed Incounters!"

Simply Click the Button Below

OR **Go to This Page**

http://preppersliving.com/free

BONUS #2: More Free & Discounted Books & Products

Do you want to receive more Free/Discounted Books or Products?

We have a mailing list where we send out our new Books or Products when they go free or with a discount on Amazon. Click on the link below to sign up for Free & Discount Book & Product Promotions.

=> Sign Up for Free & Discount Book & Product Promotions <=

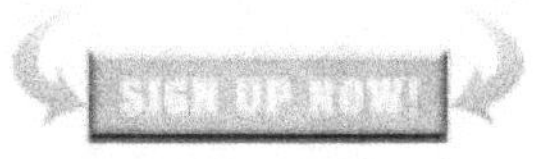

OR Go to this URL

http://zbit.ly/1WBb1Ek